Byron

versus

Elgin

Greeks and Britons together
can restore the Parthenon Marbles
and safeguard Newstead Abbey

by

Ken Coates MEP

Paper for the Byron Conference
Athens, April 1998

Byron versus Elgin

Ken Coates MEP

During the social tumult in the British coal industry, from the Great Strike of 1984 down to the wholesale closure of mines in the 1990s, there were innumerable human casualties. Large numbers of mine workers became unemployed, but unemployment also spread out beyond the coalfields, into those industries which had previously survived as suppliers to the mining industry, and those other industries which had provided services which made it possible for the mines to operate.

With mass unemployment we saw an ugly growth of poverty, indebtedness, and social disintegration. A large part of my political activity has been concerned with these problems, and I have written about them extensively elsewhere.

But there were other casualties, and the full roster of them is not yet complete. The environmental consequences of pit closures can be very complex. Subordinate ancillary industries, coking plants and chemical refineries, may close, leaving behind them horrendous problems of contamination and pollution. Under the ground, the accumulation of mine waters often dissolves dangerous substances, which may then be leeched into the surface waters, and contaminate them. Serious risks to public health may ensue. And frequently there is a problem of subsidence, which sometimes fractures and breaks up not only buildings, but whole eco-systems. All these risks existed while the mines were working, but once they had closed it became much more difficult to mobilise the resources to deal with them, and to take action to prevent them.

In Nottinghamshire, one of the by-products of these massive

1

social upheavals has been the transfer of ownership from a public corporation, the National Coal Board, to a number of private mining companies, at the same time that planning law has undergone serious changes. New, smaller, private corporations often operate on very tight margins, and find it difficult to take a broad view of their public obligations.

Although the National Coal Board had itself suffered during its later years from increasingly parsimonious policies which at times restricted its role as a public benefactor, it had, nonetheless, over a long period, distinguished itself by extensive scientific and environmental researches, and by a more enlightened attitude to public planning than certain other corporations have shown.

It was within this context that the Midlands Mining Company eventually took over the responsibility for the Annesley Bentinck colliery, and decided to extend its underground workings into the vicinity of Newstead Abbey. The new company works on narrow margins. It extracts coal from the Tupton seam and the Yard/Blackshale seam. The future of the colliery depends on continuous Eastward working from the pit-head at Annesley out to the nearby villages of Ravenshead, Linby and Papplewick. The area in question includes a considerable part of Newstead Abbey and its grounds.

The flux in planning law appears to give coal operators the right to work such areas as these without needing separate planning permission. If this interpretation of the law is right, then the planning authority, Nottinghamshire County Council, is powerless to control these mining developments, whatever damage they might entail for any historic buildings they might jeopardise. Newstead was directly in the line of advance of the projected colliery workings, and there were real fears that undermining it could cause serious damage to the buildings, possibly even collapsing them.

This was the problem which gave rise to the campaign to save Newstead Abbey, the ancestral home of Lord Byron. Newstead Abbey had been expropriated from the Church by King Henry

VIII with the abolition of the monasteries, an early exercise in privatisation which had confiscated church property and handed it over to a rising class of private gentry, who would thereafter, it might be hoped, support the Crown. This prototype privatisation also represented a frontal attack on the institutions of 16th century welfare, since the monks had hitherto provided such relief as there was for the poor. Part of the spoils of the dissolution fell to the Byron family, which took over Newstead Abbey, a foundation of Henry II from the year 1170. Sir John Byron, Lieutenant of Sherwood Forest, was the beneficiary. His descendants fought with King Charles I during the Civil War, and were expropriated by the Puritans. But the restoration of King Charles II also restored the Abbey to the Byron family, which was raised to the peerage in reward for its loyalty to the throne. The fortunes of the Abbey declined with those of its owners, until Lord Byron, the poet, inherited the peerage and the crumbling Abbey together. Byron's tenure was short, and the Abbey was subsequently taken over by others and restored with care, until it became an asset of Nottingham City Council, which has ever since maintained it as a cultural centre and recreational facility.

But to under-mine the Abbey would be to risk the destruction of a significant historical memorial, and even the under-mining of the extensive grounds would risk damage to a rich inheritance, of man-made lakes, waterfalls and ponds, and specialised gardens and water gardens. Today, these give pleasure to the citizens of Nottingham, and nearby towns, for whom they are a magnet for family outings. But theatre companies have also homed in on a perfect natural venue. And, of course, the house itself is a strong reminder of the legacy of Byron, the site of a major permanent exhibition on the poet and his life's interests, and the natural centre for national and international organisations like the Byron Society.

That was why I decided to try to extend the well-organised campaign of British supporters, and seek help in Greece, to prevent possible destruction of the Abbey and the Byron museum. I wrote to all the Greek Members of the European Parliament, and received a virtually unanimous response. The concern was spontaneous, and not at all confined to one political Group. All the Greek Members wrote strong appeals to the British Government, seeking the intervention we had been unable to secure from that quarter. Soon, there was news of meetings, petitions and ascending protests, from every part of Greece.

It was at this point that I realised that it was necessary that solidarity should engender reciprocal support. With the Greek people so impressively united in defence of the heritage of Lord Byron, did we not need to elicit a matching response in Britain to the continued theft of the so-called 'Elgin' Marbles in the British Museum, taken from the Parthenon shortly before Byron's own first visit to Athens?

Lord Byron and Lord Elgin were contemporaries, and I soon discovered that there were closer connections between the heritage of Byron and the infamy of Elgin than I had thought. As a young man, Byron, like so many other British noblemen, embarked upon the Ground Tour, culminating in his visit to Albania, Greece and Turkey. It was with profound shock that he realised the extent of the damage to the greatest treasures of Athens, and with disgust that he learnt that the worst offender was neither ancient Barbarian nor modern Turk, but his own compatriot, Lord Elgin, recently Ambassador in Constantinople, who had 'bought' the Parthenon frieze from the Turkish occupier, and carried it off home to Scotland.

John Watkins published his biography of Byron in 1822. It is, Michael Foot tells us in his own book on *The Politics of Paradise*,

> 'Libellous . . . the first in a large library of similar concoctions – in which the biographer asserted that a set of writers were assembling in Pisa to produce a new journal . . . to help form "an academy of blasphemy", and "a poetical school of immorality and profaneness".'

Watkins' book may well have been the first of many which traduced the poet: it was also, perhaps, the first of many which were widely unread by future generations. But nonetheless Watkins had

The Parthenon, 1826, in use as a Turkish arsenal

an interesting story to tell about the relations between Lord Byron and Lord Elgin.

Byron arrived in Athens during his first tour of the Near East in the years 1810 and 1811. He was

> 'greatly mortified and thoroughly indignant to see the place dismantled of many of the beauties which had rendered the spot, even in its dilapidated state, sacred in the estimation of all travellers who possess any reverence for the genius of antiquity'.

Watkins reports that the ravages of time, 'and those committed by Barbarians', were puny compared to the spoliation recently perpetrated 'in the name, and by the orders of an English Ambassador at the Porte'. Lord Elgin had 'exerted his influence so effectually as almost to demolish several of the finest of the temples that were then remaining'. As if this were not enough, the same

The Temple of Poseidon, where Byron carved his name on a column

nobleman had had his own name inscribed on a pillar of the temple of Minerva. His wife's name had also been written there. The inscriptions were most conspicuously engraved, 'at a considerable elevation'. Lord Byron was scandalised by this presumption, and had himself hoisted up to the inscription, where he 'obliterated the name of the Earl, but gallantly left that of the lady untouched'. But since inscriptions were in fashion, he then went to the west side of the same temple, and etched, in large letters,

> 'Quod non fecerunt goti,
> hoc fecerunt Scoti.'

Whatever Byron wrote on these ruins of Athens, however, his indignation found a more permanent outlet in his poem *Childe Harold*, parts of which were for a long time suppressed because they were deemed 'too caustic for publication'.

Unfortunately, Byron took *Childe Harold* to the publisher William Miller, who rejected it because he also published the writings of Lord Elgin and found that Byron's criticisms of his other author were too sharp. Subsequently John Murray not only published *Childe Harold* itself, but also brought out *The Curse of Minerva*, which went far beyond the earlier poem in its onslaught on Elgin.

> 'So let me stand through ages yet unborn,
> Fix'd statue on the pedestal of scorn
> Though not for him alone revenge shall wait,
> But fits thy country for her coming fate.'

Minerva's curse, provoked by the spoliation of the Parthenon, and the theft of its Marbles, charges the British with tyranny, and threatens them with the retribution of the oppressed.

> 'Look to the East, where Ganges' swarthy race,
> Shall shake your tyrant empire to its breast;
> Lo, their rebellion rears her ghastly head,
> And glares the Nemesis of native dead
> So may ye perish! Pallas when she gave
> Your freeborn rights, forbade ye to enslave.'

Loot, war and oppression were not only to be visited on victims overseas. At home in England there was a virtual civil war, involving the frame-makers and the Luddites, and raging all round Byron's seat at Newstead Abbey. Byron could identify a tyrant empire which offered ruthless repression not only in the cradles of ancient civilisations but also up to the borders of his own estate.

The development of new machines for textile production had caused widespread distress in the North of England, reaching down into the Midland Counties. Independent manufacturers were squeezed out of business by the growth of machinofacture, and unemployment became endemic. There arose an extraordinary resistance. Organised gangs, under the banner of King Ludd, or Ned Ludd, who may have been an imaginary figure, began a series of audacious night raids, breaking up the new machines, and burning down the factories in which they were installed. In the beginning, the Luddites attacked only the machinery which was displacing them from work. But in 1812, a group of Luddites was shot down, at the request of an employer. Afterwards he was murdered. And as the riots spread, severe repression bore down on the insurgence, and at a mass trial in York, in 1813, many people were sentenced to death or transportation. The mood was graphically expressed in a letter left in Chesterfield Market Place, which has survived in the Home Office papers:

> 'I ham going to inform you that there is Six Thousand men coming to you in Apral and then We will go and Blow Parlement house up and Blow up all afour hus labring Peple Cant Stand it No longer dam all Such Roges as England governes but Never mind Ned lud when general nody and his harmy Comes We Will soon bring about the greate Revelution then all these greate mens heads gose of.'

The mayhem surged over Nottinghamshire, and Byron found, on his return to that County that

> 'not twelve hours elapsed without some fresh act of violence; and on the day I left the County I was informed that forty Frames had been broken the preceding evening.'

Ned Ludd appears in womens clothing

It was in response to this impasse that a Framework Bill was tabled in Parliament. And it was in the debate on this Bill that Byron intervened, with his passionate statement in defence of the Luddites:

'When we are told that these men are leagued together, not only for the destruction of their own comfort, but of their very means of subsistence, can we forget that it is the bitter policy, the destructive warfare, of the last eighteen years which has destroyed their comfort, your comfort, all men's comfort; – that policy which, originating with "great statesmen now no more" has survived the dead to become a curse on the living, unto the third and fourth generation!

These men never destroyed their looms till they were become useless – worse than useless; till they were become actual impediments to their exertions in obtaining their daily bread . . . an you wonder then, in times like these, when bankruptcy, convicted fraud, and imputed felony, are found in a station not far beneath that of your Lordships, the lowest, though once most useful, portion of the people should forget their duty in their distresses, and become less guilty than one of their representatives?

But while the exalted offender can find means to baffle the law, new capital punishments must be devised, new snares of death must be spread for the wretched mechanic who is famished into guilt. These men were willing to dig, but the spade was in other hands: they were not ashamed to beg, but there were none to relieve them. Their own means of subsistence were cut off: all other employments pre-occupied; and their excesses, however to be deplored or condemned, can hardly be the matter of surprise.

I have traversed the seat of war in the Peninsula; I have been in some of the most oppressed provinces of Turkey; but never, under the most despotic of infidel governments, did I behold such squalid wretchedness as I have seen since my return, in the very heart of a Christian country . . .

Setting aside the palpable injustice and the certain inefficiency of the bill, are there not capital punishments enough on your statutes? Is there not blood enough upon your penal code, that more be poured forth to ascend to heaven and testify against you? How will you carry this bill into effect. Can you commit a whole county to their own prisons? Will you erect a gibbet in every field, and hang up men like scarecrows? Or will you proceed (as you must, to bring this measure into effect,) by decimation; place the country under martial law; depopulate and lay waste all around you, and restore Sherwood Forest as an acceptable gift to the crown in its former condition of a royal chase, and an asylum for outlaws?

Are these the remedies for a starving and desperate populace? Will the famished wretch who has braved your bayonets be appalled by your gibbets?

Mr Wynne

late foreman of a jury held
at nottingham 16 march - 12
Sir,
by General Ludds Express Express
Commands I am come to
Worksop to enquire of your Character
towards our cause and I am sorry
to say I find it to correspond with
your conduct you latly shewed
towards us, Remember the
time is fast aproaching when
men of your stamp will be
brought to Repentance, you may
be called upon soon. Remember
you are a marked man
your for Genl Ludd
a true man

Letter from General Ludd to the foreman of a Nottingham jury

When death is a relief, and the only relief it appears you will afford him, will he be dragooned into tranquillity? Will that which could not be effected by your grenadiers, be accomplished by your executioners? If you proceed by the forms of law, where is your evidence? Those who refused to impeach their accomplices, when transportation only was the punishment, will hardly be tempted to witness against them when death is the penalty.

When a proposal is made to emancipate or relieve, you hesitate, you deliberate for years, you temporize and tamper with the minds of men; but a death-bill must be passed off hand, without a thought of the consequences.'

BYRON: speaking in the House of Lords against the Frame-breaking Bill, 1812.

When they are informed about this powerful statement, English schoolchildren set it in a long-distant historical context. Times and manners have changed: but there are some issues in Byron's speech which retain a burning relevance. Machines are still displacing people in the modern economy, on a scale which is all the more remorseless for being based on advanced science and high technology. But unemployment and rejection are no more acceptable to excluded people in our century than they were in the days of Lord Byron.

Bertrand Russell recognised that Byron spoke for a revolutionary epoch. The poem *Don Juan* expressed that epoch so sharply that Russell felt compelled to include a chapter on Byron in his *History of Western Philosophy*, even though the poet has not normally been described as a philosopher, and even though Russell had a great love for the other heroes of the Romantic Movement, most notably, for Shelley, who did not feature in his *History*.

'Sorrow is knowledge; they who know the most
Must mourn the deepest o'er the fatal truth.
The tree of Knowledge is not that of Life.'

But it is power which decouples knowledge from virtue, and alienates science from humanity. Today, that imperial power confronts us in the extreme alienation of nuclear weapons, which threaten to destroy mankind and all its works. Does this threat issue from knowledge alone? Of course not. It comes from the secretion of knowledge in the constraining mould of power.

Byron knew this when he enlisted himself in the cause of Grecian liberty. This was no narrow national engagement. Over and again he protested his admiration for things Turkish, and clearly insisted that his enemy was not an ethnic entity, but a form of oppression. The theft of the Parthenon Marbles was also a form of oppression.

Elgin was a soldier diplomat, and a notable empire builder. His son was to go on to a lifetime of distinguished service of Queen

Newstead Abbey

Victoria, soon to become the Empress of India. It took the oppressed masses a little longer to rise up and claim their 'long arrear of northern blood', than Byron thought. But the symbolism of *The Curse of Minerva* remained the more powerful, for the durability of wrongs which it denounced.

Empire endured for more than a century after Byron died. The stolen Marbles remain in the British Museum until the present moment. And the Luddites gave place to the British trade unions, who have not recovered their freedom to operate even at the end of the Twentieth Century. So the legacy of Byron is still important for freedom everywhere.

That is why it is important not to let Newstead Abbey collapse, and not to leave the most exciting monument of Greek civilisation immured in the cold vaults of the British Museum. The tree of Knowledge may not be that of Life, but as far as any of us can tell, freedom remains indivisible.

Printed by the Russell Press Ltd. Tel: (0115) 978 4505.

Published in 1998 by Spokesman, Bertrand Russell House, Gamble Street, Nottingham, NG7 4ET. Tel: (0115) 9708318. Fax: (0115) 942 0433.